## *Praise for the writing of Stephen Vicchio*

"Posing initially as a Neil Simon send-up of
Jean-Paul Sartre, *Ivan & Adolf* gathers (a
clandestine) momentum, moving from the
trivial to the visionary. What begins in
vaudeville ends in revelation."

Sarah Fenno Lord
Theater Critic

"Should Hitler rot in hell for eternity?
Before you say 'yes,' read this play—
a hellaciously funny, devilishly clever,
demonically disturbing discourse on
the nature of forgiveness."

Michael Davis
Editor, *Baltimore Jewish Times*

"Stephen Vicchio has created a provocative
exploration of the problem of evil, condem-
nation, redemption, and mercy through the
dialogue of two unlikely souls—presided
over by wisdom. This drama is full of
intriguing challenges."

Dr. Dorothy M. Brown
Professor of History, Georgetown University
Interim President, College of Notre Dame of Maryland

"[There is] no higher praise than to compare Vicchio's expression to Loren Eiseley and Annie Dillard at their best."

*St. Anthony's Messenger*

"The thought of extending even a shred of forgiveness to Hitler is anathema to me. Nevertheless, Stephen Vicchio seems to lead us to a provocative conclusion: That the line between when it is morally perverse to forgive and when it is virtuous to do so is a very thin one indeed."

Rabbi David Fohrman
Senior Editor, Mesorah Publications' elucidated
*Babylonian Talmud*

"Stephen Vicchio has that rare thing, a finely-tuned sense of style, and it is employed with the happiest of results."

Josephine Jacobsen
Poet, former poetry consultant, Library of Congress

"Vicchio is a national treasure..."

Ramsey Flynn
Editor, *Baltimore Magazine*

KEVIN     DUNMIRE

# Ivan & Adolf

# Ivan & Adolf

## THE LAST MAN IN HELL

*A rather dark comedy
or a perhaps hopeful tragedy
in three acts and nine scenes*

## Stephen Vicchio

WOODHOLME
HOUSE
PUBLISHERS

*Baltimore, Maryland*

Printed and bound in the United States of America.

1 2 3 4 5          06 05 04 03 02 01 00 99 98 97

**Library of Congress Cataloging-in-Publication Data**

Vicchio, Stephen.
   Ivan and Adolf : the last man in hell / by
   Stephen Vicchio
       p.    cm.

   ISBN 0-9656342-9-9    (pbk. : alk. paper)
   1. Hitler, Adolf, 1889–1945—Drama. I. Title.
PS3572. I245I93  1997
812'.52—dc21                              97-9322
                                             CIP

Woodholme House Publishers
1829 Reisterstown Road
Suite 130
Baltimore, Maryland 21208
Fax: (410) 653-7904
Orders: 1-800-488-0051

*Book design:* Brushwood Graphics, Inc.
*Cover illustration and design:* Nancy Johnston

*For Jean*

"Hell is other people."

Jean-Paul Sartre
*No Exit*


"What is hell? The suffering that comes
from the consciousness that one is
no longer able of love."

Feodor Dostoyevski
*The Brothers Karamazov*


"There shall not abide eternally in the
fires of hell a single believer, but whoever
has in his heart the weight of a single
grain of compassion eventually shall
be brought forth."

Al Ghazali
*Ihya*


"Hell is oneself. Hell is alone, and all
the other figures in it merely projections.
There is nothing to escape from and
nothing to escape to, one is always
alone...The final desolation of solitude
in the phantasmal world of imaginations,
shuffling memories and desires."

T.S. Eliot
*The Cocktail Party*

# Table of Contents

# Characters

*Sophie (a maid)*

*Ivan Karamazov*

*Adolf Hitler*

*Two Moving Men*

Before the play opens
Alexander Nevsky's
"Field of the Dead,"
Opus 78, plays softly in
the background.
• • • • • • • • • • • • • •

# Act I

# Act I

***The Time and Setting:*** *Much like that of G.B. Shaw's "Don Juan in Hell" scene from his* Man and Superman: *No light, no sound, no time nor space, utter void.*

***The Scene:*** *A large apartment in Hell, some-time in what those who live on earth would call the distant future. Three Victorian couch-es (in the color and arrangement of those in Sartre's* No Exit*) dominate the drawing room. The middle couch (CS) is empty. It is well-worn, dusty, barely functional. Seated on the couch to (SR) is Adolf Hitler. He is dressed in his field uniform from 1945, the year of his death. To (SL) is seated Ivan Karamazov. He is dressed in the manner of an 1850s Russian intellectual. Both men wear appropri-ate hats that hide unsightly head wounds. Hitler is listening to a portable stereo set with head phones, while Karamazov reads a fully*

3

*opened newspaper, behind which he is partial-
ly concealed. To the extreme (SR) is a set of
French doors, leading to an off-stage bedroom. To the rear (SL) is a small kitchen. On
both ends of the kitchen are large wooden
pantries.*

*Behind Ivan and Adolf, in the center of the
back wall, is a large wooden door held slightly
ajar by Sophie, a black maid. Sophie is dressed
in a housedress and long apron. She carries a
feather duster in her left hand. Her right arm
hugs the edge of the open door. She appears to
be saying farewell to someone whom just
moments before has made his exit.*

SOPHIE: *[Calling out the door.]* You be careful now, Genghis. You remember your man-
ners when you get up there. You keep an
eye on that temper of yours, and you mind
the cutlery! If you don't watch yourself,
you'll be the first one who's ever made a
roundtrip. *[She closes the door, and leans
back against it, clutching the feather duster
to her chest.]*

*[Absentmindedly.]* Lord knows I thought
that man would never make it. *[She looks
toward the couches, where both men sur-
reptitiously have been watching. When
she catches them, they both resume their
activities, pretending to ignore Sophie.]*
Thought he would never get that temper
under control.

*[She begins to dust the empty couch
between the two men.]*

*[To herself.]* This place sure does collect a

lot of dust. Every time I turn around, there is more of it. Who would have thought dead people could make such a mess? Well, I guess the management will be sending someone down to pick up this old dust catcher. One thousand years that man sat there, calling himself the "Master of the Mongols," wanting me to wait on him hand and foot. Who would have thought he'd have made it before either of you two?

ADOLF: *[Putting down the head phones.]* I still say he was faking it.

*[Ivan immediately peers over the top of his newspaper.]*

That man was not nearly as sorry for what he has done as I have been. I've seen lots of them come and go. Some arrived a lot later than I did; some left a lot less penitent. For over two hundred years I have been stuck in this place. In the beginning, I admit, I had a lot to learn. I waited for my head wound to heal. I made the best of that series of rabbis I was given as roommates. But in two hundred years I have yet to get a single hearing about my release. I am sorry...if I could just talk to someone in charge, someone in the management, I'm sure I could show them how much I have changed.

IVAN: *[Folding the newspaper and rising.]* Do you think your little display of contrition is going to work? I don't believe you, and I'm not even omniscient. You are right about one thing, I don't think that Genghis "Khan-artist" was sorry either. And even if he were, after what he has done how can anyone, even Him *[he looks up]* forgive such a black heart? You complain about being here for only a few hundred years, after the evil and destruction you have wrought? I'm afraid if God is just, your stay here is going to be an eternal one. You should make yourself comfortable, eternity is not long enough punishment for the likes of you.

SOPHIE: *[Still dusting.]* This is exactly what keeps you both here. The place is entirely cleaned out: Pope Alexander VI, Leo X, Clement VII, Idi Amin, Richard Speck, Rasputin, Richard Nixon, O.J. Simpson, the Menendez brothers...and now Ghengis Khan...they all are gone, and you two still sit here going at each other. In the meantime, some a whole lot worse than either of you got to working on themselves and, before you know it, another hundred years or so and there they go—they make it out of here.

IVAN: Sophie, we have talked about this a thousand times. *[He rearranges himself on the couch.]* I am perfectly content to wait. Eventually, justice will be served. If He *[looking up again]* really is omniscient and all good, then he will kick out the murderers from Heaven and send them back here where they belong. In the meantime, I have hastened to give back my ticket. The only satisfaction I get while waiting is knowing that He had enough sense to keep "Mein Führer," here, exactly where he belongs.

*[While Ivan makes this comment Adolf moves to the large mirror SL.]*

ADOLF: *[While moving.]* With all this whining of yours I could swear you are Jewish. Between your grousing about injustices and all that prattle from Khan about the superiority of the Mongol race, how does anyone ever find the time to work on oneself down here?

*[He removes his hat and stares at the wound on his right temple reflected in the mirror.]*

IVAN: Oh, time is something you have plenty of...

SOPHIE: And it's comments like those that make me think you are going to be enjoying the accommodations here for a long time.

ADOLF: *[Not listening to Sophie; he absent-mindedly fingers the oozing wound on the right side of his head.]* I really do think it is getting better, don't you Sophie? You know when your wounds are finally healed that's the first real sign you'll be leaving soon. Remember that American writer who was forever telling those hunting and fishing stories, and those ungodly books of his he insisted on reading aloud—such ugly short sentences. Well, toward the end he got very quiet; seemed much more at peace with himself and those around him. Then the wound on his head began to disappear. The next thing you know...he's gone. I really do think my wound is looking better.

IVAN: *[Breaking in.]* How could such a sniveling little worm almost own the entire planet? It's hard to believe you were a man that very nearly ruled the whole world. You're pathetic. Now Khan, he took over his father's empire when he was thirteen. Napoleon? He actually led troops into battle. And remember Alexander, the tall Greek fellow? He left a few years ago. Now there was a leader. No easy way out for him. *[He stares at Adolf. Making his right hand into a pistol he pretends to shoot himself in the right temple.]* Alexander died in a drinking contest! One might almost think he was Russian.

ADOLF: I sustained this injury in a scuffle in my bunker. I was shot by one of my subordinates. It happened in the throes of a death struggle, an heroic struggle for the gun. A fire had started in the bunker. We were forced there by the allies' advance. There was confusion. We were preparing an important plan for regaining the territory we had lost. Some of my underlings wished to give up the struggle, but I insisted that we push on. The man who shot me had lost his courage to continue.

IVAN: Is that why you've had powder burns on the side of you face for over two hundred years. That little thing in your temple is a small contact wound. You didn't even have the courage to use a large caliber pistol. You're right about one thing: The man who shot you had lost his courage to continue.

*[Adolf moves back to his couch. Ivan moves to the mirror.]*

Now this is head wound. *[He removes his hat.]* I pulled the trigger. I intended it. At the end of my life I fell ill with fever and delirium. My father had been murdered by another man, one of his many illegitimate children. He had it coming to him; I had wished to do it myself, but Smerdyakov beat me to it. Later Smerdyakov gave me the money he had stolen from my father's house during the murder. He told me that I had given him the idea for killing the old devil. He said that I had insisted that everyone in the Karamazov household would be better off without the ruthless old man. But, by a series of odd coincidences, all the evidence at the time pointed to my brother, Dmitri. We knew the next morning the trial would begin. The outcome was all but decided before hand. Dmitri would be shot or hanged. That's probably why Smerdyakov hanged himself the night before the trial. He felt guilty about framing Dmitri. I think he was expecting me to do the same.

Later in the evening, the night before the trial, the Devil appeared in my room and told me there was only one way out for me as well—I would have to make a sacrifice. One could argue, I suppose, that Smerdyakov was right. I was just as responsible for the murder as he was. The Devil pointed out that if I killed myself, the jurors would think we had formed an intimate conspiracy to kill my father; perhaps this would be enough to allow Dmitri to go free. So I did it. And I used the kind of gun that would get the job done...a big gun! Now this is a head wound.

ADOLF: But it was not your fault because this Devil made you do it.

IVAN: The Devil did not make me do it. He simply pointed out that there was a way of saving Dmitri's life.

ADOLF: And that's why you did it?

IVAN: Yes, it was for my brother. It was an act of courage, the exact opposite of what you did hiding in that bunker. Mine was a selfless act. You were in that bunker in the first place because you are a coward. You were hiding, Hitler. You shot yourself because you could not face what the future held for you. Mine was an act of protest, an act of familial altruism; yours was a display of cowardice. One act has nothing to do with the other. The only similarity is that they both went bang, and my bang was a considerably larger one than yours.

ADOLF: And I suppose your various fist fights and the other disgraceful behavior since you've been here all came as a product of your great altruism. That distasteful incident in the ballroom back in 1996 happened, I suppose, because of that strong vein of selflessness that runs through you as well.

IVAN: I'm not sorry about what happened in the ballroom. Sirhan Sirhan should not have been dancing with Marilyn Monroe. I don't care how sorry he was. I saw Lee Harvey Oswald standing off to the side like a moonstruck teenager. All those people had forgotten why they were here. If I hadn't cut in and thrashed that Turk, who knows what might have happened?

ADOLF: Well, because of your altruism the ballroom is closed and, with the exception of dear Sophie *[he looks at her]*, you are the only human contact I am allowed these days.

SOPHIE: It's your only human contact because you are the only two left in this ungodly place. Men...men...men! They are always talking about how tough they are. Remember that American who left a few weeks ago, G. Gordon Liddy? Walking around Hell putting cigarette butts out on the palms of his hands. Why after a while, I just told him to grow up and behave himself. A few years later, it finally dawns on him. Why would you want to be a tough guy in Hell? Then—poof!—he seems to get it. After a while, he's helping Charley Manson with his crossword puzzles. He and Ivan Boesky start that aerobics class; they organize a few dances...

ADOLF: *[Interrupting.]* When the ballroom was still open...

SOPHIE: A few more years go by and Mr. Liddy develops new skin on those burnt palms of his. Then the management thought it was time. Next thing you know, I'm making him a box lunch for the trip. If he could make it, why can't you, Ivan? A soul might think you'd leave that testosterone back on earth where it belongs. Who you going to kill down here, Ivan? Adolf? Everybody's already dead, and now they're gone, too. Whole thing seems pretty silly to me. You must begin to work on yourselves down here. This can be an awful place when you do nothing but think about yourself.

*[Lights fade.]*

Between the first and
second scenes the music
of Gustav Mahler
should be played.
• • • • • • • • • • • • • •

# Act I

## S C E N E   T W O

*The Scene: Later (in the sense that anything
is "later" in Hell). The apartment remains
essentially the same with the exception of the
couch (CS), which has been removed. Ivan sits
on his couch (SL). He plays with a small chess
set. Adolf sits (SR), playing with a hand-held
computer toy that whirs and buzzes as the
scene opens. For the first several moments of
the scene, Adolf plays with some gusto, while
Ivan unsuccessfully attempts to concentrate
on his game.*

*[Ivan makes several side-glances at Adolf.]*

IVAN: Do you suppose you might turn that
thing down? I thought that one of the con-
solations of being dead was that a fairly
large parcel of silence came along with it.

ADOLF: I enjoy these games. They keep

13

me sharp. They help to pass the time. I should think that in your great selflessness you might not mind a bit of noise if it helped another to forget about his suffering for a while. Besides, I wouldn't worry. When you are here all by yourself it will be quiet enough. You'll be a very lonely soul, Herr Karamazov, and you will grow to hate the silence.

IVAN: I will never be here all alone, nor will you, mein freünd. You will have lots of company when God returns the fakers and the charlatans to Hell, where they belong. Then, He will give me my rightful place, a place of honor, and you will be surrounded by others like yourself: the Bulgarian soldiers who tore babies from their mothers' arms; your flunkies Himmler, Mengele, and the rest of them; Po Pot; Raskalnikov; Svengali; Joseph Stalin; Hannibal Lector. They all will be back. Then you can play video games together for all eternity. Then you can make as much noise as you want.

ADOLF: [Moving to the mirror.] When my wounds heal [he gingerly touches his head] you will be a very lonely man. And your inability to forgive will be the ultimate source of that loneliness. You think that the last man in Hell will be the killer of ten million people—Jews, Gypsies, cripples, homosexuals—that God is some kind of cosmic statistician. Perhaps the last man in Hell will not be the greatest mass murderer of all time, but the man who was too self-righteous, and too self-absorbed, to forgive

him. You wear your indignation like a
badge, Karamazov. It is like a neon adver-
tisement for your considerable virtue.

*[Enter Sophie. She is dressed in winter hat
and coat and carries two large grocery bags.
Both Ivan and Adolf move quickly to aid
her with the packages. She hands the contents of the sacks to them, and they put the
provisions away in separate pantries, Ivan's
(SL) and Adolf's (SR). Among the contents
of the shopping bags are Hellman's
Mayonnaise, devil's food cake mix, hot
peppers, deviled eggs, deviled ham, etc.]*

SOPHIE: I have never seen it like that at the
company store. Fresh fruit, vegetables, my
choice of cuts of meat...no one around...it's
like the whole place has turned into a ghost
town in a matter of centuries. Except, of
course, this apartment. Hell really is empty.
There's talk they're going to change the
place into an amusement park, or maybe a
museum. You remember Jim and Tammy
Bakker? They reconciled while they were
here. Now they are thinking about buying
the place—a sort of tourist attraction for
the people in Heaven. Another rumor has it
that Donald Trump wants to come back
and buy it, or possibly Leona Helmsley, or
maybe Michael Jackson. He wants to turn
it into a petting zoo.

There's lots of talk among the management
about you two as well. They say you're like
two folks living in shacks while the ground
around you is condemned. Great new

palaces go up all around, but you two are busy arguing about where your property lines begin and end. You never seem to notice that you could be living as kings. The management's thinking they may have to remodel the place around you. It seems so sad to me. All it would require is a bit of kindness...you put a few acts of kindness together and soon it becomes a habit. After a while, you become surprised at the person you have become. *[She roots in the first bag.]* Who gets the red hots?

ADOLF: Those are mine, and those hot peppers, too. *[He places them in his pantry.]*

SOPHIE: Do you really think, Ivan, that any of those roommates you have had were any easier to get along with than Adolf?

IVAN: It was quite a collection, wasn't it Sophie? The Marquis de Sade...Blue Beard...that baseball player...

SOPHIE: Who gets the mayonnaise? *[She holds up a jar of Hellman's.]*

ADOLF: That's mine as well.

SOPHIE: *[To Ivan.]* Ty Cobb.

IVAN: Right...Ty Cobb. And that clown...

SOPHIE: John Wayne Gacey.

IVAN: Wouldn't take off that red nose, no matter what I did; parading around here in that clown outfit. Then there was Robert Irsay; remember, he wanted to move the volley ball team to the other side of Hell.

Then there was Ted Bundy...Jeffrey Dahmer...J. Edgar Hoover...a couple of decades with L. Ron Hubbard...and then that senator...

SOPHIE: *[Unpacking.]* Jesse Helms or Strom Thurmond?

ADOLF: I had Strom Thurmond.

IVAN: Yes, I had Senator Helms...and Senator McCarthy. You had Thurmond and Kennedy. What a collection of weak-willed cry babies. I could write a book about them. *[Ivan watches Sophie pull something from the bag.]* The deviled eggs are mine...and the hot cross buns.

SOPHIE: And you think that Adolf was any worse a roommate than any of them were?

ADOLF: *[Oblivious.]* I ordered the deviled ham.

IVAN: Yes, in fact I do. Ted Bundy was a faker, but he was a great faker. I think that's what got the man a transfer. In the beginning he was not so subtle, wearing that fake plaster-of-Paris cast so I would do his laundry. But by the end, he had an air of studied sincerity that was vaguely attractive. Certainly more than vaguely attractive to you *[to Sophie]* and the management; after all, he's not here any more. Now my new roommate *[he looks at Adolf who has moved to the table where he begins to prepare a sandwich]* is a faker, but he's a failure at it. I guess one could say he is a faker at being a faker. The only one he has managed to convince of his goodness is himself. And so he sits here, befuddled about why the management can't see what a good job he's done of being sorry. Now you must understand, I have a certain amount of admiration for good fakers. My father was like that. But I have nothing but disdain for Herr Hitler.

ADOLF: *[Who has not been paying careful attention. He spreads the Hellman's on the deviled ham.]* I wrote a book once. It won a good number of awards. I might have had a literary career had I not made the sacrifice to rid the world of...*[he looks at Sophie]* I mean had I not been, well, misguided about the methods for improving the world. I know now, of course, that I was wrong. I might have gone about my plan in a more constructive way; nevertheless, I take full responsibility for unfortunate things that took place on my watch. Mistakes have been made in my administration.

SOPHIE: He learned that use of the passive voice while rooming with Richard Nixon.

ADOLF: One of the more interesting of my cohabitants, I must say. In fact, with the exception of a few of the rabbis, Richard Nixon was the only one of my roommates who wasn't surprised when he woke up in Hell. The rest were very disappointed: Harry Truman, William F. Buckley, Louis Farrakhan, Oliver North, Redovan Karadzic...they all could be a bit surly, particularly when they first arrived. This is not the easiest place to get used to. Boy, were they upset when they got here. It wasn't easy in the beginning getting along with them. I liked them, though, and I got along with most of them quite well, which is more than I can say for my current situation. *[He stares at Ivan.]*

IVAN: Herr Hitler, you are a pathetic creature. That the killer of thousands, perhaps millions of children could characterize his life as—how did you put it?—"misguided," might well lead one to believe that you are more evil than the Devil himself...and certainly far more deluded.

SOPHIE: All this talk about the Devil... Beelzebub...Satan...Beliel...the Deceiver... the Prince of Darkness...Lucifer...the Antichrist...the prince of Demons! You seen him around here lately, fellas? Even he's gone—left on Thursday—the last of the fallen angels made it up there before either one of you did.

You know, after the world came to an end...

ADOLF: *[Interrupting.]* Yes, the atomic war. Seems silly to have called those other two skirmishes "world wars," doesn't it? They sure were wrong about the big one. It was with a bang...not a wimper.

SOPHIE: Yes...after the big bang, we had a population explosion around here. Satan was very happy in those days. He really enjoyed all the company. Suffering seems so much easier for some folks when they think that others are suffering even more than they are. But after things started thinning out down here, Satan became moody, a little preoccupied. Then he had that accident on the skating rink...his feet got caught in the ice. The more he batted his wings the colder the ice got. The colder it got, the thicker it got; the thicker it got, the more he batted his wings. Stayed that way for eons. Sound familiar to anybody? *[She looks at the two men.]*

Eventually, Lucifer—I heard he's gone back to his old name—figures out that maybe the key is to stop trying so hard. He stops flapping and he starts paying more attention to the people still left down here. He starts giving people who happen to walk by advice. He's got lots of time so he begins to spend it on others. Next thing you know a few millennia go by, his feet thaw out, his heart follows, and—poof!—he's out of the ice. In a matter of no time at all, he's got his old job back as the Prince of Light in the heavenly court.

ADOLF: In some ways I'm really glad he made it. At least now people will stop calling me the "Devil himself."

IVAN: He'll be back...you'll see. He *[Ivan looks up]* has some kind of plan where, in the end, he'll eternally punish those unforgivable ones. He is merely toying with them now...perhaps giving them a good idea of what they will be missing eternally. You'll see. God acts in mysterious ways, and I'm going to be around when it all makes sense. In the meantime, I'm perfectly content to sit here. *[He picks up the newspaper and opens it so he is no longer visible.]*

SOPHIE: You know another sign that you'll be leaving this place soon? You cease to be preoccupied with yourself. I have seen it happen down here a million times. Now look at the two of you...with your devil's food cake, red hots, deviled eggs, hot cross buns...you can't be released from Hell until you begin to release yourself from your obsession with getting out of this place. You can't live in Heaven until you have learned how to keep this place from being any more difficult than it already is.

Haven't either of you ever stopped to wonder why we all speak English down here? And the torture chambers...haven't you ever asked why there are no torture chambers in Hell?

IVAN: I thought that was the purpose of cable TV.

SOPHIE: There are no torture chambers here because you two have been placed together for a purpose. Do you remember that Frenchman, the thin fellow with the mustache and the wandering eye?

ADOLF: You mean the one who got in the scuffle with Albert Camus a few May Days ago?

SOPHIE: That's the one! He had it right, yes

sir. If you can get along with each other...no, you have to do more than that...if you help transform each other, despite the fact you could not dislike each other more, then there is still hope. If you cannot, then it is clear your purpose in being here is nothing more than to serve as hell for the other. There is a wonderful irony in this. God either uses you to regenerate the one you hate the most, or God uses the other to torture you for eternity. Either way, God is acting through you, but the paradox is that you must decide. You must decide Ivan, the gates of Hell are locked from the inside.

*[Lights fade.]*

Between the second
and third scenes the
music of Thomas
Dorsey's 1932 record-
ing of "Precious Lord,
Take My Hand" should
be played.

. . . . . . . . . . . . .

# Act I

## S C E N E   T H R E E

*The Scene: The same apartment, years, per-
haps centuries later; little has changed. Ivan
sits on his couch (SL). He reads the biblical
book of Job. Adolf sits on the far end of his
couch (SR). He is reading* How to Win
Friends and Influence People. *Sophie enters
with a vacuum cleaner in her hands. She
moves to see what Ivan is reading.*

SOPHIE: Ah, the book of Job. A little light
reading? *[She moves to read over Adolf's
shoulder.]* How to win friends and influence
people...

ADOLF: I have decided I am entering a self-
help phase in my rehabilitation. *[He pulls
out a collection of other books from behind
the couch, reading off the titles.]* How to Be
Your Own Best Friend; Men Are from
Mars, Women Are from Venus; The Road

23

*Less Traveled; Building Word Power; The Celestine Prophecy; Imagining a Slimmer You; The Autobiography of Dale Carnegie; Twelve Steps to Effective Stress Management; Thirty Days to Buns of Steel;* and *When Bad Things Happen to Good People.*

*[He piles the books around him.]*

I have decided that my real problem is I have not yet been able to forgive myself. That's the real key...one must start with forgiveness of oneself. I am going to get in touch with my feminine side...my inner child. I've been neglecting my left brain. I am embarking on a holistic journey of self-discovery. If I can't be my own best friend, then I can't expect anyone else to love and respect me. I can't expect anyone else to be my friend. The real key to my rehabilitation is understanding that I am a victim myself.

IVAN: *[Who has begun to listen.]* And the babies and mothers...the old men and women you had killed? Where does their forgiveness work into the equation? Did you even give them time to forgive before you butchered them? Did you allow them to pray before the shower doors were closed. Did they have time to forgive or be forgiven? Were they given time to atone for their sins, or to say a simple good-bye? What kind of victim were you compared to them?

*[Softer.]* There was a young French woman with her four-year-old daughter. One of

your guards told me this story not all that long ago. Where was your feminine side when it came to them? She was in the line with the little girl for the gas chamber showers. The guard stopped the two at the head of the line. They would be the first to enter with the new batch.

ADOLF: I don't want to hear this story.

IVAN: *[Talking over Adolf's objection.]* The little girl and the mother were stripped of their clothing. The mother pretended to be brave, but the child instinctively knew that something was amiss...

ADOLF: Please, no more...

IVAN: *[Again speaking over Adolf.]* No...you must hear this! She squeezed her mother's hand tightly as they waited for the great iron door to reopen. When the door finally swung open, the girl smelled fear in the air. She stared into the dark chamber and said to her mother: "Mommy, I'm frightened... it's dark in there, and I've been so good."

*[Adolf moves to his couch and pretends to read one of the self-help books.]*

*[Harder.]* You want to talk about victims? Those are the victims, and that little girl's father and grandparents who would never again see her run or play, or skin her knee in a children's game. The future that might have been hovered like a ghost over the rest of their lives. Those are the victims! The notion that you see yourself as a victim is

the sickest part of this sham of justice. You want to get in touch with your inner child...try getting in touch with the feelings of those children you murdered. You are guilty Hitler—perhaps the most guilty man who ever lived. I hope you rot down here...all alone...forever.

ADOLF: *[Putting down the book.]* I think your problem is that you are in denial. You really need to begin to search your heart, Ivan. You need to get in touch with your feelings. You need to get in touch with your higher power. I don't think we should communicate until you begin to get in touch with your anger.

*[Adolf puts on his portable headphones and sits at his couch. For the remainder of the scene he ignores the others.]*

SOPHIE: *[Moving to center stage.]* You talk a lot about justice Ivan, but you never mention the word "mercy." Has it no place? Is there no room in your heart for mercy? Is there never a point at which we must agree to forgive? Or do we embrace hatred for an eternity? Is hatred better, Ivan, when we clothe it in justice? Or is it still hatred with a good looking suit on?

IVAN: *[Thumbing through his bible, as if he is looking for something.][To himself.]* Here it is...The gospel tale of the laborers in the vineyard, the version in Saint Matthew.

SOPHIE: One of my favorite stories.

IVAN: How can it be a favorite? The landowner pays the laborers who arrive at the end of the day the same amount as those who had been working all day in the hot sun.

SOPHIE: Yes.

IVAN: But it was unfair...grossly unfair.

SOPHIE: Is that what the story is about? Fairness?

IVAN: I would say it is about unfairness.

SOPHIE: Unfairness to whom?

IVAN: To those who worked all day in the searing heat.

SOPHIE: Did they not receive at the end of the day what the landowner originally had promised them?

IVAN: Yes, but the others—those who came at the last hour—got money for work they did not do. They received what they did not deserve. It was unfair.

SOPHIE: Do you remember what the landowner asks the grumbling workers at the end of the tale? He said, "Are you envious of me because I am so generous?" Is that your problem? Are you envious Ivan?

IVAN: Of whom?

SOPHIE: Of God.

IVAN: Is that what you think? Is that why you think I am here? Because I am envious of what a nice person God is? Do you think I envy God's largesse?

SOPHIE: Perhaps something like that.

IVAN: I am not envious of God. I am angry with Him!

SOPHIE: Angry about what?

IVAN: Angry that scoundrels like Hitler won't be suffering in Hell for all eternity! Angry that some souls cram for finals. I am angry that God has a statute of limitations...that fairness disappears when forgiveness comes too easily...that justice is forgotten with the signing of peace accords. I am angry that murderers and rapists enjoy the rewards of Heaven while I remain here to rot. I am angry that in this cock-eyed universe it is beginning to look more and more like the last shall be first and the first shall be last.

*[Lights fade.]*

Before the second act
begins three minutes of
the opening of Rimsky-
Korsakov's first sym-
phony should be
played.
• • • • • • • • • • • • • •

# Act II

# Act II

*The Scene: The same apartment in Hell, months, perhaps years, decades, or even centuries later. The lights are dim and remain that way throughout the scene. But for the furniture, the apartment appears empty. Offstage (R), through slightly ajar French doors, the faint sound of snoring can be heard in the beginning of the scene. Ivan enters through the rear door. He appears drunk. He carries several bottles of vodka in his arms. He reels around the set, dropping the bottles here and there. One bottle apiece remains in each hand. Ivan speaks incoherently in Russian. He sings parts of the Russian Orthodox mass. Finally, he settles on Adolf's couch. The bottle in his right hand is open.*

IVAN: [*He removes a few self-help books from beneath him. He looks at them for a*

31

*moment and then tosses them in disgust.]*

*[He mumbles.] Care of the Soul...ugh.*

*[He settles in.]*

Ah...even his couch is more comfortable than mine. This really is quite nice. Already I'm beginning to lose responsibility. Hitler has sat here long enough that his evil spirit has even stained the cushions...huh, so has his cowardice... *[He drinks.]*

*[Ivan stares at the bottle and begins to affect a German accent.]*

You see my family tragedy has always been alcohol. I suffer from a disease...no...no... I suffer from an incurable disease. It haunts my body and soul. I am powerless to overcome my addiction. Ah...I do like the sound of that.

*[He drinks again and picks up the discarded book.]*

I, too, am a victim. All are innocent because all are victims...to be human is to be a victim. Oh, I like this very much. A life of epilepsy, alcohol, insanity, gambling, sexual obsession, insomnia. What could you expect from me? *[He looks up.]* It all could not have been otherwise. I am not responsible. *[He tosses the book away.]*

*[Ivan rises from the couch and moves (CS).]*

*[Without the German accent.]* If only it were that easy. If only one could lose responsibility by pretending it was not

there. *[Changing moods.]* What do you want me to do? I know you are watching. Who is it I am to forgive—that snoring imbecile in the next room who sleeps like a baby, not once thinking of the babies he has killed? Is it Hitler I am to forgive...he who has not lost a single night's sleep since he arrived here? What do you want with me...I who have not had a restful night in hundreds and hundreds of years? *[He drinks.]*

Or is it you I am to forgive? *[Again he looks up.]* Am I weighing on your conscience? Am I keeping you up at night? *[While hurling the empty bottle across the stage.]* Do you hurl empty vodka bottles across the universe? Do you know or care if they hit anyone?

Is my refusal to capitulate an embarrassment to you? Perhaps you are repulsed by the murderers with whom you now keep company. Then send them back here where they belong...give them the punishment they deserve! *[He opens the bottle in the left hand and drinks deeply.]* Or maybe they laugh at you for your soft heart. Do you keep me here to show them what a tough guy you are? And who pays the price for this toughness?

*[Ivan's mood again shifts.]* Ah...but then there are the other deeper, darker possibilities. After all, who is really the greatest mass murderer of all time? Certainly not that charlatan in the next room dreaming of forgiveness. You kill more in an afternoon

with heart disease and cancer than he killed in all the death camps. You destroy more in an evening of automobile accidents. You maim more in a day of bad births than we have killed in all our wars. You invented Pandora's box, but you are forever changing its contents. You bring new diseases, and supply us with just enough gray matter to wonder what it all means, but never enough to make it right. Is this why you keep me here...because I know your secret? Is this sick game something you enjoy playing?

*[Ivan takes a long swig.]*

You...who are supposed to be good, no...no...all good. You construct a planet of misery...a world founded and developed on excruciating pain. What was the name of the tree Adam and Eve were not supposed to eat from? The tree of the Knowledge of Good and Evil. What didn't they have before they ate the fruit? Presumably, the knowledge of right and wrong. What kinds of people don't have the knowledge of good and evil? Small children...imbeciles...drunkards. How could they have known what they were doing? They couldn't. Then you punish them eternally, and the rest of us along with them. That was a cute trick. Who made up the rules of this game? Why is it fair that you are both a player and the referee? And why, whether we wish to or not, must we all play this perverse game?

*[He drinks.]*

I admit, in most lives pain is less frequent than pleasure, but pain is infinitely more powerful and durable. One hour of pain in its purest form far outweighs a day, a week, a month of pleasure. Who is it that will not buckle under the onslaughts of a single tooth ache? How many of us will not cave in at the first sign of protracted pain? And who is the architect of this cock-eyed world of suffering? Who has constructed this intricate sphere of woe? Maybe it was an infant deity, or a drunken god, or perhaps a god with an exceedingly bad attitude...

Do you remember the answer you gave Job?

*[In* basso profoundo:*]*

"Who is this that darkens counsel by words without knowledge? Where were you when I laid the foundations of the world? Tell me if you have understanding. Who determined its measurements? Surely you know. What supports the pillars at its base? Who laid its cornerstone when all the stars were singing with joy in the morning, and the sons of God in chorus were chanting praise? Who pent up the sea behind closed doors, when it wept tumultuous out of the womb, when I marked the bounds it was not to cross and made it fast with a bolted gate? Come thus far, I said, and no farther:  Here your proud waves shall be stade."

What drivel! Are we suppose to love you because of your power? How is that differ-ent from the other murderers and sadists with whom you now keep company? Are you better than they because it all works out in the end? Do only divine ends justify the means? Or is it that you are a bully—a bully who gets to make up the rules and then call himself "All Good"?

Did you watch us on earth like we were wounded minnows in a giant fish bowl, your big mean eyes pressed up against the sides of the glass? Did it give you pleasure? Did you justify yourself by saying it all will work out in the end? All is for the best in the best of all possible worlds. What rubbish! And what if it all will work out in the end. What if we all are to live happily ever after. Why must we suffer so much to purchase our tickets? How could this be the best of all possible worlds? Give me the raw materials and your power, and in an hour or two I could construct a better one.

*[He drinks very deeply.]*

Or perhaps there is yet another secret. Perhaps you are a bumbler, like my new roommate, only with a bit more courage and smarts. Maybe the universe went out of control and this strange Rube Goldberg device of a plan of yours is all you could piece together. Is that why I am here... because I know about your ineptitude? Rather have me rot in Hell than spill the beans? Haven't quite lived up to your potential, big boy?

*[He takes one more long swig. His mood dramatically seems to shift again.]*

What is it...? What do you want from me?
If I am to rot for all eternity with him *[he
looks in the direction of the French doors]*,
why do you torture me in the meantime?
Does he not bring me enough suffering?
Does he not mock, every day, the very idea
of my goodness...?

And why must we speak this incessant,
ugly, language...English? Too many prepo-
sitions...the verbs always in the wrong
places...ugh...

*[He throws the second bottle across the
stage.]*

Is it not enough that I must bear his company? Is it not enough that I must share this
tiny parlor with evil itself? What do you
want from me? Just let me be. Just let me
be...

*[Ivan begins to stagger again around the
room. At the scene's end he collapses on his
own couch. One of the full vodka bottles
serves as a pillow. The others are strewn
around the floor. Ivan's arms are splayed.
His hat covers his face. He mumbles again,
in Russian, lines from the Orthodox mass.]*

*[Lights fade.]*

Between the first and
second scenes music
from Vaughn Williams'
"Job" should be
played.

• • • • • • • • • • • • •

# Act II

## S C E N E   T W O

*The Scene: The same apartment, the follow-
ing morning. Sophie stands in the kitchenette
(SL) preparing breakfast. Ivan is unconscious
on the couch, where he remains for the rest of
the scene. An afghan has been pulled over his
legs and midsection. The vodka bottles have
been cleared away. Adolf enters (SR) from the
French doors. He inhales the morning air and
stretches. He crosses the stage, examines Ivan,
lifts the Russian's right arm which immediately flops back off the couch to its original position.*

ADOLF: *[He lifts Ivan's hat from his face.]*
One might almost think he was dead...*[He
laughs, amused at his cleverness, and then
replaces the hat.]*

Good morning, Sophie...*[Adolf moves to*

*buss her on the right cheek.]*

SOPHIE: Good morning, Adolf. Did you sleep well?

ADOLF: Yes, very well...like a baby. *[He stretches again.]*

SOPHIE: I've made your favorite breakfast...cream chipped beef.

ADOLF: Ah, "sheist on der shingle"! That's what we used to call it back in a more heroic time, the Great War. I do love it so.

*[He moves back again to examine Ivan. He lifts the Russian's hat, and for a moment looks intently at his head wound. He touches it with his fingers and seems content with its oozing character. A moment later, he replaces the hat and pulls the afghan up over Ivan's neck. He stares at it for a second or two—looks to see if Sophie is watching—and then readjusts the afghan so that it covers Ivan's face.]*

*[To himself.]* There...much better.

SOPHIE: *[Not looking at Adolf.]* He's already dead, Adolf...and he's not going anywhere. Come now and eat your breakfast.

*[She moves to the table (SL), which has been set for breakfast. Ivan also moves to the table. While Sophie serves the meal, Ivan stops briefly to examine his head wound in the mirror. When he reaches the*

*table, Adolf begins to eat voraciously. Sophie, with empty pan in hand, stares at him disapprovingly.]*

ADOLF: *[Feeling her disapprobation.]* Oh, right...*[He puts down his fork and knife, folds his hands, and says a perfunctory prayer in German. Then he resumes the meal.]*

*[With food in his mouth.]* This is the third time this week. *[He points with his fork in the direction of Ivan.]* I think he needs a good twelve-step program. He needs to get in touch with his higher power. He needs to confront the demons within.

SOPHIE: Yes, he certainly is a mess...no better, really, than the day he came here. Such a tortured soul, and yet, so full of goodness. Many of the Russians we have seen come through here had the same kind of sensibilities: Tolstoy, Gogol, Pushkin, Chekov, Ivan's own brother, Dmitri—but none quite so bad as he. Or should I say none quite so bad about his goodness.

*[Adolf seems disinterested in the conversation. He makes various noises all suggesting his meal is being consumed with great enjoyment.]*

ADOLF: You know, Sophie, I think you are a classic "enabler." I have been meaning to talk to you about this for a while now and, under the circumstances *[he looks at Ivan]*, this looks like a good time. I know you think you are helping him, but you are just an enabler. In the long run you are making things worse for him...and for yourself.

SOPHIE: Oh...I see.

ADOLF: All this love and affection you bestow on Ivan...do you really think it is good for him? You are playing into the very conditions that produced his dependence, Sophie...that makes you a codependent. You continue to create the environment for his failure. It will only cause more suffering in the long run.

SOPHIE: And what would you have me do, Adolf? Perhaps I could join the Adult Maids of Alcoholics.

ADOLF: No...I think you should try "tough love."

SOPHIE: Tough love?

ADOLF: Yes, I've been reading about it. It's a way of getting Ivan to admit his dependency. You basically ignore his attempts to manipulate you into being nice to him. This forces him to be alone with his addiction. You have to let Ivan hit rock bottom before he can begin his process of recovery.

SOPHIE: Yes, that's the "tough" part...but what's the "love" part? Do you know what love is, Adolf? Have you ever been in love? Has anyone ever loved you?

ADOLF: I don't know. My people loved me, Sophie, and I loved them. Have you never seen *Triumph of the Will*?

SOPHIE: Was it "love," Adolf? Or what you call "co-dependency"? The sadist needs the victim. The strong need the weak just as much as the weak need to hide behind the strong. Which were you, Adolf? Were you the weak or the strong?

ADOLF: Perhaps you have forgotten, but for a bit of bad weather and a few miscalculations by my subordinates, I would have ruled the entire world. My name is still mentioned along with Napoleon's, Charlemagne's, and Bismarck's.

SOPHIE: And they all are gone and you are still here. You do suffer from a kind of addiction, Adolf...but it is one for which you are entirely responsible. You are addicted to self-deception. You need to stop running from yourself...you run so fast, you look like Jesse Owens.

ADOLF: Sophie!

SOPHIE: Sorry, Adolf, I know that remains a touchy subject for you. There is no one here to watch you now...no one to convince...your only watcher is Ivan, and he's not buying what you are selling. You can't keep developing cardboard versions of the self and expect Ivan to love one of them. You won't stop trying to deceive, Adolf, until you cease deceiving yourself.

ADOLF: What's that suppose to mean?

SOPHIE: It means that the self you have fashioned, your soul, is too small to be found. There is nothing there to be

admired. It's all in miniature like those tiny
figurines in a Christmas train garden...little
tiny roads and cars...teeny little houses
where tiny little people live. They're too
small, really, ever to be alive. They're too
small to have a real soul. You are in danger,
Adolf, of the self disappearing completely.

ADOLF: In Germany, during my administration, the trains always ran on time.

SOPHIE: Yes, even the trains to the death
camps. You are still running, Adolf, but
where are you going to hide in Hell? The
whole place is closed down. All of Hell has
been emptied out except this small apartment. All you have is Ivan...all he has is
you.

ADOLF: I have you, Sophie.

SOPHIE: This is not about me, and you
know it. You must prove that there is someone there, someone behind those eyes of
yours—those eyes that always look for
what the other is thinking of you. Forget
about your own concerns, Adolf, concentrate on the "other," and the soul will get
larger. Continue to concentrate on yourself,
and the self will disappear, and you will be
here forever.

ADOLF: It's not that simple, Sophie.

SOPHIE: It is that simple, but first you must
understand how much suffering you have
caused. You must understand why Ivan
may never forgive you. You first must construct a self that is capable of understanding

that. You must fashion a self that is capable of shame, but, more importantly, you must first make a soul that is capable of feeling guilt.

ADOLF: And God, Sophie? What of God?

SOPHIE: God cannot forgive you until there is someone there to forgive...

ADOLF: And if God is not capable of forgiving that self?

SOPHIE: God is capable of forgiving every self.

ADOLF: Does everyone deserve forgiveness, Sophie?

SOPHIE: Forgiveness is a gift. It's revenge that's predictable. Revenge is the natural, automatic reaction to being deeply hurt. Forgiveness is an entirely creative act. It comes out of nowhere. It is completely unpredictable. For most human beings, it is incomprehensible. It is as close as humans come to creating something out of nothing—the same way God made the universe.

ADOLF: Do I deserve forgiveness, Sophie?

SOPHIE: It's not a matter of deserving. For your part, it is a question of constructing a self that is large enough to be forgiven.

ADOLF: Is it possible for me to be forgiven?

SOPHIE: It is possible for anyone to be forgiven.

*[The lights fade with Sophie wrapping her arms from behind around the seated Adolf.]*

Between the second and third scenes three minutes of Schubert's unfinished symphony should be played.

· · · · · · · · · ·

# ACT II

*The Scene: A few days later, a Sunday, Sophie's day off. Ivan and Adolf sit on their respective couches. Ivan again reads the newspaper. Adolf sits with his hands folded in his lap.*

ADOLF: I hate Sundays.

*[Ivan continues to read.]*

I said, "I hate Sundays." When Sophie has a day off there is no one to talk with...nothing to do. Hell is so ungodly boring on Sundays.

*[Ivan looks over his paper at Adolf.]*

IVAN: I don't care what you think about Sunday—or the rest of the week for that matter. What difference does it make what day it is in this place? Why don't you find a

47

new hobby that would require you to be out of doors more often? It would be much better for both of us, I think, if you occupied yourself with something other than talking to me. I have no use for you Hitler, and I have no use for what you think about Sunday. Please, leave me alone. This could be so much more endurable for the both of us if you just let me be.

ADOLF: Suit yourself. *[Adolf moves to the kitchen area.]* I just thought it would be good if we tried to understand each other a little better.

IVAN: You thought it would be good? What would you know about goodness? You want us to understand each other? My problem with you does not stem from my inability to understand you—indeed, just the opposite...I understand you only too well.

ADOLF: And what is it that you understand about me, Ivan?

IVAN: I understand that you are a worm, and by some strange act of collective hypnosis you managed to convince millions of people that you were an heroic human being. You put on that uniform, you held a number of impressive parades, you gave some heroic speeches...but still, you were only a worm...a worm pretending to be a hero. And you still are a worm now.

ADOLF: Perhaps you are right.

IVAN: What?

ADOLF: I said, "perhaps you are right." I
am a worm, but can you also understand
that I feel?

IVAN: Did you "feel" when you were
slaughtering ten million people?

ADOLF: No, but I feel now.

IVAN: And what is it that you "feel," Hitler?

ADOLF: I feel what you feel, Ivan. I feel your
hatred for me. It is palpable. I feel it all
day...every day...for hundreds, perhaps
thousands of years. I feel the pain you have
about God being so distant. I feel the lack
of hope you felt when you shot yourself,
but, I admit, I did not feel your courage. I
felt the rage you felt at your father, I felt it
toward my own. I feel your deep loneliness.
I feel the terror that runs through you like a
live electrical wire. I feel the fear you have
in giving up what you have held most dear.
I feel what it is like to be utterly alone...a
loneliness of my own making. I know more
about what you feel than you may think.

IVAN: And do you feel what your victims
felt?

ADOLF: Until now, no.

IVAN: And now?

ADOLF: [Breaking.] And now a day does
not go by, an hour does not pass, that I do
not think about it...about them. I think,
Ivan, that you are right. It is quite fair, quite
just as you would put it, that I be the last

man in Hell. I am a worm, but I am a worm
trying to make himself into a human
being—not a hero, just a human being. I
don't know if I ever will complete the
project. I wish for mercy, but I am willing
and able to accept justice.

IVAN: And the source of this great realiza-
tion?

ADOLF: It was mostly Sophie...the constant
attention...her selflessness. After decades
and decades it began to sink in. She has
helped me to construct a self that does not
spend all its time thinking about itself. You
have helped me too, Ivan, in an indirect
way. You have helped me to stop thinking
about myself. Perhaps you have helped me
to find out that I didn't have much of a self
there.

IVAN: And what do you spend your time
thinking about now with this newly found
self of yours?

ADOLF: I spend my time thinking, and at
night I spend my time dreaming, about the
children. This is what Hell is, Ivan: Feeling
deeply and being powerless to do anything
about it. That's why we are both still here.
I seek forgiveness, but I deserve justice. You
seek justice, but you deserve forgiveness.
You wonder about the justice of God. I
wonder if I ought ever be forgiven for what
I have done.

IVAN: I can't do it. Don't ask me to forgive
you. I cannot, I will not, give up my anger
about you.

ADOLF: It is not your forgiveness I seek. I
   seek it from God, and from those whom I
   have murdered and their families. From you
   I seek friendship. I seek the friendship of a
   fellow lonely sinner, someone who suffers
   like you do.

*[Adolf moves to (SL). He holds his hand
out to the seated Ivan. Ivan stares at the
hand. For the briefest of moments Ivan's
hand moves to meet Adolf's, but then with-
draws a moment later. Ivan exits through
the rear door, slamming the door behind
him.]*

*[Adolf collapses on Ivan's couch.]*

*[Lights fade.]*

For three minutes before the opening of the third act Ray Charles' 1956 recording of "Drown in My Own Tears" should be played.

• • • • • • • • • • • • •

# Act III

# Act III

*The Scene: The same apartment, months, perhaps years or decades later. The set remains the same with the exception of the large mirror (SL) which has been removed. Ivan sits at his couch (SL), playing chess. Sophie cleans the evening's dishes.*

SOPHIE: *[Wiping her hands with a dish towel.]* Well, that's about it, Ivan. I'll be heading home for the evening. Adolf has gone out for a walk. He said to tell you he would be down by the old ball room, if you were looking for him. *[She moves to get her hat, coat, and a Company Store shopping bag from one of the kitchen chairs (SL).]* I'll see you in the morning, God willing.

IVAN: *[Looking up from his game.]* An odd expression, Sophie. Do you really think God cares a wit about what happens to us down here? Do you think our welfare sits right at the front of his omniscient mind? Consider the lilies of the field...every little fallen sparrow. Aren't those the lines? Do you really think that God wills everything for the good; that he carefully orchestrates all that happens?

SOPHIE: Yes, I do.

IVAN: Then He is like a sadistic child playing with his ant farm. Do you think that God willed for Hitler to murder all those people?

SOPHIE: No, I don't. I think human beings have no idea what God is thinking. I think the real God is not the God of the philosophers.

IVAN: And what is He the God of?

SOPHIE: God is the God of love, the God of mercy and forgiveness.

IVAN: And the God of justice?

SOPHIE: Yes, justice tempered by mercy and forgiveness.

IVAN: And what is this mysterious virtue, forgiveness?

SOPHIE: [Smiling at Ivan.] Last week Adolf brought me some violets...you've seen them...they bloom just inside the west gate of Hell. [She moves to look at violets arranged in a vase on the kitchen table.]

After a few days one of the heads of the violets fell to the floor. In my running around

here all day, I inadvertently stepped on it,
unwittingly lodging the violet between the
heel and sole of my shoe. For the remainder
of the day I could smell the sweet fragrance
of the violet. At first, I thought it was the
violets in the vase, but I continued to smell
the sweet fragrance throughout the day—
even when I did the laundry, when I went
shopping at the Company Store, and after I
had gone home for the night.

Later in the evening, when I was undressing
for bed, I discovered on the bottom of my
shoe the source of so much of the day's
pleasure—the crushed violet. A moment
ago you asked what forgiveness is. Ivan,
forgiveness happens when the violet lends
sweet fragrance to the heel that crushes it.
In his own way, this is what Adolf has
begun to understand. You have seen it in
him, Ivan, I know you have. He needed to
learn what guilt feels like, the gnawing
kind; you need to learn to forgive. If you do
not, you will continue to burn the same
bridge over which you must travel to return
home.

IVAN: Do you think God will forgive Adolf?

SOPHIE: God forgave Adolf a long time ago.
It's Adolf that needs to be convinced of it,
not God.

IVAN: And if I am not convinced by his
goodness?

SOPHIE: Adolf's or God's?

IVAN: Both.

SOPHIE: You don't need to be convinced, you need to be loved.

IVAN: By God or Hitler?

SOPHIE: Perhaps by God through Adolf. For you to love God, Ivan, you need God to have a human face. You must begin to understand God as having the most human of faces. Adolf's is the only human face you have left.

IVAN: But you have a human face, Sophie. *[He thinks for a moment.]* Has anyone ever told you that you are very clever for a maid.

SOPHIE: It's really very simple, Ivan—you need to be loved.

IVAN: I don't need to be loved. I need to be answered.

SOPHIE: And just what kind of answer would satisfy you? That God is as vengeful as you are; that God's inability to forgive matches yours? Maybe God's love is the answer. Maybe that's the only answer there is...

Have you noticed that Adolf's head wound has begun to heal? Since the mirror was removed, he scarcely mentions it. It won't be long now, Ivan. You have seen the difference in him. You know what he has made of himself down here. He has learned how to feel...to love. He has made it possible to be loved. You must decide. You must decide if you will be going with him. You must decide if you can give up the anger, if you may learn to forgive.

IVAN: And the past, Sophie? Must we bury the past and pretend by a sheer act of the will that it never happened? We could think of it as a cosmic badminton game and just declare a let. Should we give them all a clean slate: Hitler, Mussolini, Albert Desalvo, the Moors murderers, the Kray twins, Adolf Eichmann? Must we affect a clever kind of amnesia where everyone gets to start over? Ought we turn the moral odometer back to zero?

SOPHIE: [Putting on her hat and coat.] The past means little in eternity. God gave people memory for healing, not just for wounding. Is it better to live in an eternal present or a dead and painful past? I don't think you know.

You are fond of quoting Job's speeches, Ivan. You like those tortured lines of his...his clenched fist raised against the heavens...his Promethean outbursts...his railing against the great inequities. But do you remember when God asks him at the end of the book: "Is it by your wisdom that the hawk soars, and spreads its wings toward the south?"? Is it by your wisdom, Ivan?

IVAN: Is it God's power or His goodness you are in love with, Sophie?

SOPHIE: I think that's what you need to

decide, Ivan. You need to decide whether you can believe in a God whose goodness includes mercy. You must decide how much goodness is to be found in God's power. You know, you act like a man stranded in the desert who takes it in his head that his whole vocation is intentionally and defiantly to pour the only available water through a sieve. You need to decide if you will continue to waste the water, Ivan; perhaps it is time to see if you are ready to drink it.

*[Lights fade.]*

Between the first and second scenes three minutes of Alexander Nevsky's "Field of the Dead" should be replayed.

. . . . . . . . . .

# Act III

*The Scene: The apartment, a few weeks, perhaps months or years later. Sophie arranges violets in a vase on the kitchen table. Her hat, coat, and shopping bag are on a chair by the door. Ivan sits at his couch, reading Augustine's* Confessions. *After a moment, he looks up and notices Sophie, and then her coat and bag.*

IVAN: *[Closing the book and pressing it against his chest.]* So...tomorrow's your day off.

SOPHIE: Yes, I do like my day of rest.

IVAN: I have not had a day of rest since I got to this place. *[He thinks for a moment.]* Where do you go on Sundays, Sophie? What do you do when you are not taking care of us?

SOPHIE: I try to rest. There is so much to do around here that I try to get myself back together on Sunday, so I can help you two the rest of the week. But it's gotten to be so exhausting.

IVAN: Where do you go when you leave here, Sophie? Tell me about where you live. Where do you go in the evenings when you are finished with the dishes?

SOPHIE: I go back home...it's actually quite far...the directions are rather complicated. I don't think you would know the neighborhood.

IVAN: Sophie, [*changing his light tone*] you don't live in Hell, do you?

SOPHIE: No, I don't. [*She pauses.*] It has taken you thousands of years to ask about me. We have spent all these years together and only now do you ask. Dear Ivan, I've been with you all this time, and finally you wonder about me. But perhaps that's a good sign.

IVAN: Do you live up there?

SOPHIE: Yes, I have quite a nice place.

IVAN: What's Heaven like?

SOPHIE: Quiet...peaceful. Heaven is full of people with nothing to prove.

IVAN: Why would you live in Heaven and work in Hell?

SOPHIE: I think you know the answer to that question.

IVAN: "Sophie"'s not your real name, is it?

SOPHIE: Yes, it is, but I am known by many different names, as well.

IVAN: Why would you come to Hell?

SOPHIE: If the Devil can go to Heaven, why can't God help out a little bit in Hell? *[She pauses.]* If you were God and all your creation was in Heaven but two lonely, fearful men, two men who so often seem bent on their own eternal destruction, even after they already live in Hell, where would you be? If all but two were enjoying the eternal happiness of Heaven, where would you be? Besides, they do fine up there without me.

IVAN: If I were God, Heaven would be a very different place—far less populated for one thing—and we'd have a three-strikes-and-you're-out rule. *[He pauses.]* Does Adolf know who you are?

SOPHIE: No. This is not about Adolf anymore. He'll be leaving tomorrow.

IVAN: Does he know about you?

SOPHIE: No, if he did, he could have been doing it for the wrong reasons.

IVAN: Does he know about his transfer?

SOPHIE: No. I'll tell him in the morning. And you? Will you be going with him?

IVAN: I don't know. Do you want me to tell you I am sorry? Is that what you want? All I always have wanted is that things should be fair...that people should be rewarded and punished for the lives they have led. Do you want me to beg your forgiveness? Is that what you want? I don't think I can do that, not even of you.

SOPHIE: No, I want you to love...and to learn somehow to forgive.

IVAN: I don't know if I can do that.

SOPHIE: I know. *[She opens Ivan's pantry. It is full of vodka bottles and various books by Kierkegaard, Kafka, Dostoyevski, Thomas Mann, Albert Camus, Dante, Milton. She reads the titles out loud.]*

Let's see: *Fear and Trembling* and *The Concept of Dread*; Kafka's *Metamorphosis* and *The Trial*; *Crime and Punishment* and *The Underground Man*; *Magic Mountain*; *The Stranger* and *The Plague*; Dante's *The Divine Comedy*; *Paradise Lost* and *Samson Agonistes*.

IVAN: *[He shrugs.]* You are what you read...*[he pulls out one of the vodka bottles and takes a deep swig]*...and what you drink as well.

SOPHIE: *[Picking up two of the books.]* Ivan, why do you insist on knowing the mind of God. These are like children's art placed on the refrigerator door. We argue too much about whether this figure is a cow or a horse. You can't draw a picture of God, Ivan. It's only finger painting. You don't think enough about the fact that it is love that's the real magnet that attaches those pictures.

You must decide, Ivan. Adolf will be leaving in the morning. You must decide if you are able to forgive. There is no hatred in Heaven, not even the righteous kind. You must decide if you will be leaving, too.

*[Lights fade.]*

Between the second and third scenes Charles Albert Tindley's 1905 version of "We'll Understand It Better By and By" should be played.

* * * * * * * * * *

# Act III

## SCENE THREE

*The Scene: The apartment, the following morning. Several bags are packed and sitting by the rear center door. The mirror (SL) has returned. Ivan sits at the kitchen table. He reads* The Diary of Anne Frank.

*Sophie answers a knock at the door. Two burly moving men enter. They are dressed in overalls with "The Company" stenciled on their backs.*

FIRST MOVING MAN: We are here about the couches.

SOPHIE: Oh, right...*[she points in the direction of the two remaining couches.]*

*[The moving men lift Ivan's couch, carry it to CS, and then reposition it. Next they lift Adolf's couch and exit with it. Ivan moves*

*to his couch, where he begins to read his book.]*

*[Adolf emerges from the bedroom. He is dressed in long sleeve shirt and dark pants. His military uniform is gone. His head wound is completely healed. Sophie's hat, coat, and bag are on the chair by the door.]*

ADOLF: *[Looking around.]* Well, I suppose I'm ready.

*[Adolf moves to touch Ivan on the shoulders from behind but stops just before making contact. Then he moves to the rear door where he picks up his suitcases and looks back at Ivan. Ivan continues to pretend he is engrossed in his book. Sophie finishes working on a box lunch for Adolf and then begins to put her coat on. Before buttoning it, she moves to (CS) and addresses Ivan.]*

SOPHIE: I'll be going too, Ivan. I'm taking a little vacation.

IVAN: *[Putting the open book in his lap.]* Where are you going?

SOPHIE: Back home for a while, but I'll be back.

ADOLF: Who will stay with Ivan? Who will take care of him?

SOPHIE: Ivan will be fine by himself. I think he prefers it that way.

ADOLF: No one prefers it that way.

SOPHIE: *[Buttoning her coat and moving toward the exit.]* Come now, Adolf, you will be late for the bus. This is the last bus out of here. The service has been discontinued. "All ashore who's goin' ashore..."

*[Adolf puts down his bags and pauses for a moment, then moves to sit on the right end of Ivan's couch. Ivan immediately moves to the far left end without putting down his book.]*

ADOLF: *[To Sophie.]* If it is all right with you, I think I will stay. There are still some things I'd like to do down here...some loose ends I'd like to help tie up.

SOPHIE: *[Moves to the rear exit.]* Why am I not surprised? I'll be back. And remember, I'm not far if you need me.

*[Sophie lingers at the door for a moment. Adolf sets up the chess set between the two men on the couch.]*

ADOLF: Would you care for a game, Ivan?

IVAN: *[He looks up from his book and pauses for a moment.]* Ah...I think not. I had planned on catching up on my reading.

ADOLF: Come, Ivan, what harm would it do?

*[Ivan closes the book.]*

IVAN: *[Hesitantly.]* What harm would it do? Perhaps you are right. I must fill the time as best I can.

*[Ivan puts down the book. Adolf finishes setting up the chess pieces.]*

ADOLF: Yes, we both have plenty of time. It's the one thing we have enough of down here. Well, then, it is your move, my friend. As Sophie would say, "The first shall be last and the last shall be first."

*[Sophie has exited quietly. Ivan and Adolf begin to study the board. As the lights fade, Albert Tindley's "We'll Understand It Better By and By" can be heard softly playing in the background.]*

*The End*

# Postscript

"A work of fiction is a mirror
dawdling down a road."
Stendahl (Marie Henri Beyle)
*De l'amour*


"The method employed is directly
calculated to deceive—egregiously
deceive—the superficial skimmer of pages."
Herman Melville, from a review of
Nathaniel Hawthorne's
*Mose From the Old Manse* (1846)


In one of his finest essays, Henry James
observed:

> The great question for the poet, the
> dramatist, or the novelist is 'How does he
> feel about life?' What, in the last analysis,
> is his philosophy? When vigorous writers
> have reached maturity, we are at liberty
> to gather from their works some expres-
> sion of a total view of the world they
> have been so actively observing. This is
> the most interesting thing their works
> offer us.

James believed that the philosophical drama-
tist ought to be concerned not only with issues
generated from the essential terms of his existence, but he also should be committed, in a
self-conscious way, to creating a work of art
that stands as an unalterable record of the
urgency of that quest, and similar quests of
other thoughtful people, living and dead.

The best of philosophical dramas ought to reveal a kind of triple bond. The absent playwright and the present theatergoer come to a meeting ground which is the play—a world created for the stage, but a world displayed so that it might be commented upon and interpreted by any who happen by and willingly enter into it. The task of interpretation is a difficult one. It is much like the job of a primitive shaman left to read the future of the tribe in the entrails of a sacred pigeon, and the results are just as important.

One way a spectator at the theater may interpret the dialogue between playwright and viewer is to see the work as autobiographical. On these terms, the drama is to be understood as referring to, or connected with, the life of the playwright. The play becomes a literal or symbolic revelation of a personal history, a kind of complicated ink-blot test exposing the mind and heart of the playwright.

Certainly *Ivan and Adolf* can be viewed from this perspective. While writing the play I was in the midst of a divorce. Accusations flew back and forth with the regularity and the bone-numbing exhaustion of transcontinental commuting. Both sides saw themselves as wronged. Both parties had, as best I can tell now, an inability to see any truth on the other side. It takes no deep understanding of psychology to see that these issues dominate the play.

But the philosophical play also must be something more than this, something greater than the ruminations of the playwright about his broken home. A good drama should tell us at least as much about the play's world, even if it is not *the* world, as it does about the playwright. In the process, it also should call to mind questions that are relevant for our world. In a good philosophical play, these questions are of the most profound kind. They are questions about the nature of reality, the definition of truth, the existence of God, the foundations of morality, the nature and limits of authority (both inner and outer) and the anatomy of virtues (intellectual and moral). These are questions that thoughtful people in every age have found it necessary to ponder.

One of the profound ironies of the latter part of the twentieth century is that these questions so infrequently are raised by, and among, professional Anglo-American philosophers. In an autobiographical statement written at mid-century, Karl Jaspers already had come to something like this same conclusion when he contrasted his experiences as a practicing psychiatrist with his life as a professional philosopher:

> The memory of the intellectual fellowship of our hospital in Heidelberg has accompanied me throughout my life. My later work in philosophy, however, was undertaken independently and at my own risk, without contact with a professional group. The comparison enabled me to measure how diffused, artificial, and unreal are the professional associations

of professors of philosophy, no matter how often its representatives may meet each other in congresses or express themselves in journals and books.

What frequently is lacking in professional discussions among Anglo-American philosophers is, for lack of a better term, an existential commitment to the big questions, or, if the adjective unnerves you, the traditional questions. In my own career, it has become increasingly obvious that it is one thing to become familiar with the vocabulary and the stock moves and counter-moves of the history of philosophy, but it is quite another to suffer from what Edmund Husserl called "the despair of one who has had the misfortune of falling in love with philosophy."

Josiah Royce in his *Spirit of Modern Philosophy* suggested that philosophy should be about the "more serious business of life." In contemporary academic circles, philosophical discussions are rarely about that business. The most direct result is that English speaking philosophers talk to themselves, and to each other, but rarely to the rest of the world; frankly, the rest of the world would find them boring.

One antidote for this condition is to read and to view the work of philosophical dramatists, men and women who create worlds in which the serious business of this world is discussed at length and depth. It must be done with attention to plot and character, but in the best of philosophical dramas these big questions are never absent from the stage. Indeed, they are the very reason for the play's existence.

In *Ivan and Adolf* I have attempted to engage the audience in a dialogue about some of the most serious business of life. I have chosen to do it by using one character with historical roots, Adolf Hitler, and another with literary ones, Ivan Karamazov. In order to avoid charges of historical inaccuracy, I have taken these two figures out of historical time and placed them in the realm of the afterlife. The claim that "Adolf Hitler would not act that way in the afterlife," seems an odd one, indeed. It is perhaps akin to an ancient Scandinavian freshly and miraculously returning from the dead to announce that Hamlet was not like Shakespeare's version at all. Could we not say, "fair enough," and then move on to talk about the timeless importance of the play, about the larger philosophical and religious issues that moved the Elizabethan playwright to borrow from the history of Denmark.

What many viewers may find difficult about this play is that I raise the possibility that even Hitler someday in the distant future might be capable of receiving forgiveness. Clearly this raises one of the major dramatic tensions of the play, a tension that resides not only in Ivan Karamazov, Hitler's protagonist in the drama, but also among many of those who read or come to see the play. Ought the worse man who ever lived receive the joys of salvation and the communion of those he has murdered?

At a literal level, I try to ask in *Ivan and Adolf*
just how long Hell ought to last. In the early
rabbinic tradition the answer to that question was an interesting one. The Babylonian
Talmud suggests that it ought to be long
enough that the sinner comes to genuine contrition. But the Talmud also points out that the
mourning prayer, the *Kaddish,* is only to be
said for eleven months after the death of a
loved one, because any person seeking forgiveness in the afterlife will by that time have come
to full reparation with God. The ancient rabbis do mention special cases where a soul's
sense of the good is so distorted it may never
come to the possibility of forgiveness. But
these souls, according to the ancient sages, disappear. They become nonentities devoured by
their own spite; they do not languish in Hell
for all eternity. In *Ivan and Adolf,* Sophie
warns Hitler in Act II that he is dangerously
close to having his soul disappear completely.
For the ancient rabbis, there are no damned
souls.

At a more allegorical level, the play raises a
couple of the central questions of the serious
business of life. Although these questions are
raised in a created world, they are also meant
to be reflected upon in, and about, this world.
These questions are simple to state. They are
incredibly difficult to answer with any authority, beyond that of personal moral intuition. Is
it worse to be a morally corrupted person, or
one who cannot forgive that person no matter
what, even if God could? Are there necessary
and sufficient conditions for forgiveness? Is
contrition one of them? Are there some acts

and people who by their very natures might forever remain unworthy of forgiveness? Is it possible to forgive without forgetting? Is it possible to forget without forgiving?

I don't know the answers to these questions. I have, nevertheless, taken a position on some of them in this play. The point of view I have taken will provoke some; I hope it will move others. More importantly, I hope it will cause those whom it provokes to speak and listen to those whom it moves.

# Acknowledgments

John Donne was correct: No man is an island. No man is a peninsula, either. The writer's ideas always come from many different directions. The playwright, the novelist, and the essayist incur a number of debts along the way. They are not always the best at expressing gratitude, for there is an ever-present problem: How does a writer know just how a particular idea became his own? Stealing is far worse in a fully conscious thief. It is a bit better in one who acknowledges his heists. I hope you will find much in this play that reminds you of ideas grown elsewhere as more impressive and robust plants—in Sartre, Shaw, Dante, and Milton, to name a few.

I am also indebted to friends and loved ones, particularly, Jean Nolan, David and Laura Duncan, Dawn White, David Fohrman, Sarah Lord, Michael Davis, Nanny Warren, Henry Silverman, and Tom Benson, all of whom read and commented on the play while it was in route to the finish line. Brian and Liz Weese, wise and generous publishers, should be praised for their uncanny love of books, something all too rare these days in the publishing business. Finally, gratitude must go to Gregg Wilhelm, who continues to be the best editor, and one of the dearest friends, I have found in the book business.